D1576162

	DAT
6/21	

Demco, Inc. 38-294

Gardens

Tools for the Garden

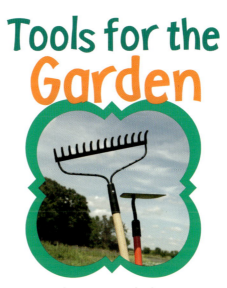

by Mari Schuh

Consulting Editor: Gail Saunders-Smith, PhD

Consultant: Sarah Pounders
Education Specialist, National Gardening Association

CAPSTONE PRESS
a capstone imprint

Pebble Books are published by Capstone Press,
151 Good Counsel Drive, P.O. Box 669, Mankato, Minnesota 56002.
www.capstonepress.com

Printed in the United States of America in North Mankato, Minnesota
092009
005618CGS10

Library of Congress Cataloging-in-Publication Data
Schuh, Mari C., 1975–
    Tools for the garden / by Mari Schuh.
    p. cm. — (Pebble books. Gardens)
    Summary: "Simple text and photographs present garden tools and how
they are used" — Provided by publisher.
    Includes bibliographical references and index.
    ISBN 978-1-4296-3983-5 (library binding)
    ISBN 978-1-4296-4841-7 (paperback)
    1. Garden tools — Juvenile literature. 2. Gardening — Juvenile literature.
I. Title. II. Series: Pebble (Mankato, Minn). Gardens.
SB454.8.S38 2010
635'.04 — dc22
                                                                           2009025591

Note to Parents and Teachers

The Gardens set supports national science standards related to life
science. This book describes and illustrates tools used in gardens.
The images support early readers in understanding the text. The
repetition of words and phrases helps early readers learn new
words. This book also introduces early readers to subject-specific
vocabulary words, which are defined in the Glossary section. Early
readers may need assistance to read some words and to use the
Table of Contents, Glossary, Read More, Internet Sites, and Index
sections of the book.

Table of Contents

4

Time to Garden

Want to plant a garden?
Gardening is easy when
you have the right tools.

Tools You Wear

Wear a hat for shade
from the sun.
Gloves protect hands
from thorns and mud.

Digging and Raking

Spades dig deep
in the soil.
They dig holes for plants
by scooping out the dirt.

Break up soil with a hoe.
Hoes chop and cut out
weeds too.

Drag a rake back and forth to make the soil even.

A hand trowel digs holes for seeds.

Watering Tools

Watering cans

gently sprinkle water

on tiny plants.

Garden hoses spray water on large areas.

Cleaning Your Tools

Always wash and dry tools

after you use them.

Put them away.

Now they are ready

for the next garden project.

Glossary

hand trowel — a small hand tool with a shallow metal scoop

project — a task or job worked on over a period of time

soil — the top layer of earth where plants can grow

spade — a digging tool with a flat blade and a long handle

sprinkle — to wet lightly

thorn — a sharp point on the stem of a plant

weed — a plant that grows where it is not wanted

Read More

Johnson, Terry. *Growing New Plants.* 21st Century Junior Library. Ann Arbor, Mich.: Cherry Lake Publishing, 2008.

Schuh, Mari. *Animals in the Garden.* Gardens. Mankato, Minn.: Capstone Press, 2010.

Whitehouse, Patricia. *Plant and Prune.* Tool Kit. Vero Beach, Fla.: Rourke, 2007.

Internet Sites

FactHound offers a safe, fun way to find Internet sites related to this book. All of the sites on FactHound have been researched by our staff.

Here's all you do:

Visit *www.facthound.com*

FactHound will fetch the best sites for you!

Index

Word Count: 112
Grade: 1
Early-Intervention Level: 13

Editorial Credits
Jenny Marks, editor; Heidi Thompson, designer; Marcie Spence, media
    researcher; Eric Manske, production specialist; Sarah Schuette, photo stylist;
    Marcy Morin, scheduler

Photo Credits
All photographs by Capstone Studio/Karon Dubke.